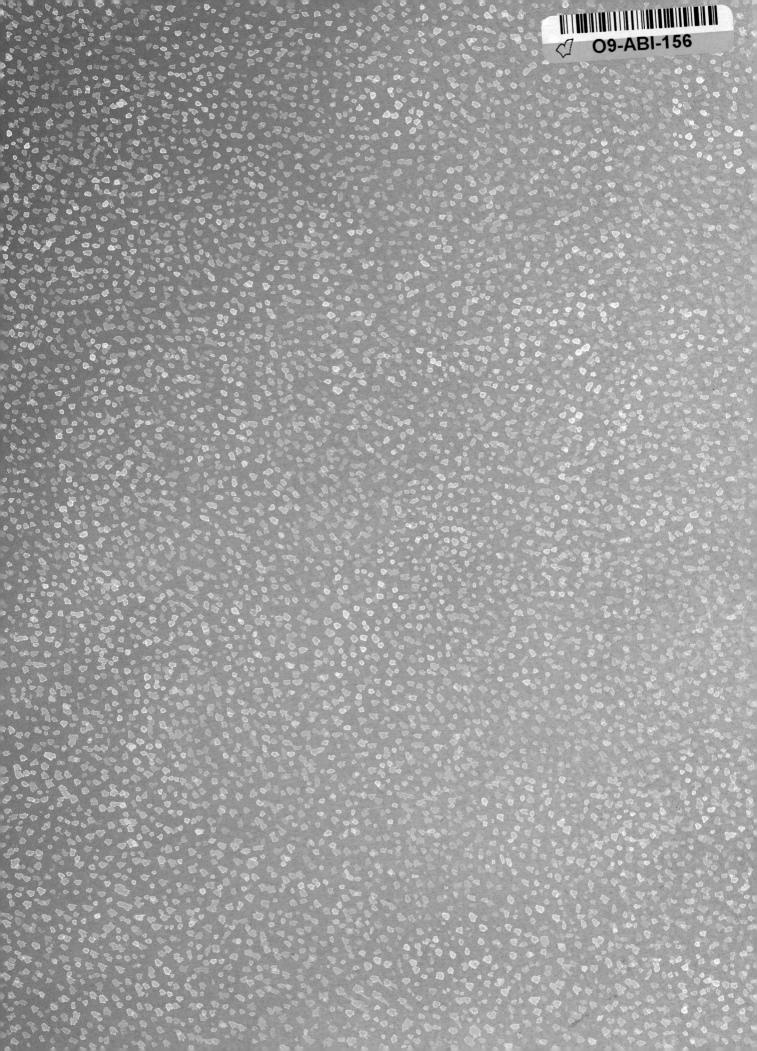

WHEN IT SNOWED THAT NIGHT

BY

NORMA FARBER

ILLUSTRATED BY

PETRA MATHERS

A Laura Geringer Book

An Imprint of HarperCollinsPublishers

When It Snowed That Night
Text copyright © 1993 by Thomas Farber
Illustrations copyright © 1993 by Petra Mathers
Printed in the U.S.A. All rights reserved.
Typography by Christine Kettner
1   2   3   4   5   6   7   8   9   10
❖
First Edition

Library of Congress Cataloging-in-Publication Data
Farber, Norma.
    When it snowed that night / by Norma Farber ; illustrated by Petra Mathers.
        p.   cm.
    "A Laura Geringer book."
    Summary: A collection of nativity poems featuring animals who travel from
afar to be at the manger of baby Jesus and protect him from the snow.
    ISBN 0-06-021707-3. — ISBN 0-06-021708-1 (lib. bdg.)
    1. Jesus Christ—Nativity—Juvenile poetry.   2. Children's poetry, American.
3. Animals—Juvenile poetry.   [1. Jesus Christ—Nativity—Poetry.   2. Animals—
Poetry.   3. American Poetry.]   I. Mathers, Petra, ill.   II. Title.
PS3556.A6W48   1993   92-27414
811'.54—dc20   CIP
                                                                      AC

To the memory of Sidney Farber, M.D. 1903–1973.
—E.F.S., S.B.F., T.D.F., M.F.

For Spenser N.
—P.M.

STORK

Over my chimney-nest
I've seen that rumoring star.
What's the news, anyway?
I've come far, far.

Kings, out of my way!
Shepherd, lower your crook.
Queens, stand aside.
I want a good, long look.

O child, I take my fill.
I bow my long stork bill.

LADYBUG

From winter sleep,
this waking day,
I crawl six-legged
to a crib of hay.
Make way! Make way!

With dainty speed
I tiptoe, red
as a pomegranate seed,
a holly berry,
a hawthorn bead.

Oh what a sight
for drowsy eyes!
In a sweet hollow
just the right size
a baby lies,

snow-whitely dressed
in his newborn best.

To think I'm
worn like a jewel,
a fiery pin,
a ruby sequin,
over his heart.

 AMEL

Bid the camel rise,
unloaded of his cargo.
He moves like a ship.

LOTH

As everyone knows,
I begin to begin to travel
when the wind blows.

From bough to bough to bough,
Single-handedly I move.
Easy if you know how.

There are swifter mammals. Let them
hurry. In my own time
I'm getting to Bethlehem.

I hang on a cross-beam
within the stable: so still
I disturb no one's dream.

I hang as I please
and to please an infant
who will learn about trees.

TURTLE TOWARD BETHLEHEM

I'm slow as molasses.
That's me, that's my nature.
From every last creature
Bethlehem-bound who passes,
I'm begging for a lift.
Lion sweeps by,
Lamb right beside him.
Camel comes loping.
I holler. I'm hoping
he'll ask me to ride him.

Please get me to the manger on time!

I need to be there
while the baby's still new.
Next summer won't do.
He's in the stable today.
Tomorrow who knows?
Amazing how fast
an infant grows.

Please get me to the manger on time!

Hello Ram, with horns in your bonnet.
How tempting your back!
I wish I was on it.

Please get me to the manger on time!

Galumphing Baboon.
Big Bull, Brown Beaver, Cinnamon Bear.
Not one with a second to spare—
not Cony, not Coon.
Who are these three?
They're Kings! They're stopping. And stooping. For *me*?

I'm getting to the manger on time!

IRAFFE

I have to bend my head
to get in at the stable door.

I like the smell of this barn,
the sound of this animal chorus,

the sight of hay and an infant—
I've never seen either before.

Let him lie on a fleece on my back.
He rides and I adore.

DOVE

What thing
should I sing,
little king?
Coo-roo?

What dear word
of a bird
should be heard?
Coo-roo?

What save love
can a dove
carol of?
Coo-roo!

PIDER

I sing no sound. I spin instead.
High in the loft above your head
I weave my quiet song of thread.

I loop my wiring silver-clear
to light your manger chandelier.
Listen! My web is what you hear.

CRICKET

Wasn't it fine
that a black-backed cricket was able
to stay from the end of September
hidden in a stable—
of all surprising places—
through most of December
in time to stand at the manger—
by chance or design—
rubbing his lyric wing-cases
that chirruped Welcome! to every
newcomer kin and neighbor and stranger
and praised the gifts three Kings were bringing,
and chirruped chirruped till every creature
must carol according to its nature
and chirruped till even the straw was singing?

 AMB

Bye, baby Jesu,
look who's come to please you,
come to doff his tawny skin
to wrap a brand-new baby in.

Waken merry. Touch and see.

Jesu, you have company.

MARY

Come and rejoice,
come pray for me,
Who holds a baby
on her knee,
and keeps him safe
for what's to be.

**H**OG

Jesu dear
I lumber near
You may yank my tail
You may pull my ear.

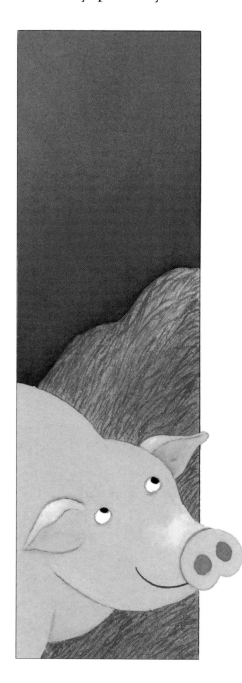

HEN IT SNOWED THAT NIGHT

When it snowed that night upon a stable,
and the roof leaked water in the hay—
Stork spread his wings across the manger,
Camel lap-lapped a puddle dry,
Coon rolled around on his back
to sponge up the drops, dripping,
Cricket clung fast to a ceiling-hole,
Dove plugged a gap with his beak,
Woodpecker pegged a tiny chink
with a right-sized splinter,
Giraffe held his head against a crack,
Spider flung his web across another,
Sloth pressed his palm against a third—
and the Three Grand Kings
raised a parasol over the family.

HE QUEENS CAME LATE

The Queens came late, but the Queens were there
with gifts in their hands and crowns in their hair.
They'd come, these three, like the Kings, from far,
following, yes, that guiding star.
They'd left their ladles, linens, looms,
their children playing in nursery rooms,
and told their sitters: "Take charge! For this
is a marvelous sight we must not miss!"

The Queens came late, but not too late
to see the animals small and great,
feathered and furred, domestic and wild,

gathered to gaze at a mother and child.
And rather than frankincense and myrrh
and gold for the babe, they brought for her
who held him, a homespun gown of blue,
and chicken soup—with noodles, too—

and a lingering, lasting cradle-song.
The Queens came late and stayed not long,
for their thoughts already were straining far—
past manger and mother and guiding star
and child a-glow as a morning sun—
toward home and children and chores undone.

# FAR, FAR FROM BETHLEHEM

I never went to Bethlehem.
I stayed right here. I plumped a goose,
put up preserves, measured a hem,
retrieved a piglet running loose.

I washed the laundry, hung it neat,
then took it down by dark of day,
and folded it and laid it, sweet
and fresh for further use, away.

I never got to Bethlehem.
Someone, I thought, should (day and night)
be here, someone should stay at home.
I think I probably was right.

For I have sung my child to dream
far, far away from where there lies
a woman doing much the same.
And neither of our children cries.